the Faerie Ring

First published 1991.

Published by
St Justin Cornwall Ltd.,
Long Rock Industrial Estate,
Penzance, Cornwall,
England TR20 8HX

Printed by Spectrum Colour Printers, St. Ives, Cornwall.

ISBN 1-872855-01-6

This book belongs to

Fairy stories are traditionally included in childhood's introduction to reading and story-telling.

Fairies abound in our heritage of literature and drama.

As the Christians adopted many of the festivals and symbols of the 'Old Religions,' so they banished the fairies as imps and demons.

Yet the 'Pagan' Christmas Tree is not complete without a fairy on the top.

fairy Godmothers, fairy Princesses, fairy Castles, fairy Cakes, fairy Lights, fairy Tales, fairy Rings, and the Tooth-fairy, are all still part of our everyday lives, and form an integral part of the natural and supernatural mythology of our heritage.

Perhaps the fair folk still live on in the more remote and sparsely inhabited regions where the old beliefs have not yet been buried forever.....

The love that faerie folk bear for children is well known. Often it is only the young, or the young at heart who have been privileged to spend time in their company

There are many tales of children who have been taken to the Hidden Realm, but the innocent have little to fear from those that dwell there.

The Faerie of the Lake

(Jan's Tale)

On a summer's evening as a small boy wandered in the meadow gathering flowers, cascades of flute-like music drifted to him from the nearby woods. He walked towards the trees, looking for the bird that sang so sweetly, across the grass and between the first trees. Gazing up into the sun dappled leaves, little Jan could see no bird, and now the music was moving away.

He followed the sounds deeper into the heart of the wood.

Brambles sprang and arched across the twisting path, nettles and nightshade waited as the light beneath the trees began to fail. Scared now, he turned to take the path home, but it was lost in the leaves and the dusk.

Then the lights appeared; sparkling pinpricks of bright colour dancing between the trees, leading him onwards. He could not see the tiny hands that held aside the bramble's thorny loops, and twitched the nettles from his way.

Deep in a hollow of the woods the lights hovered above a pool, the music softened to a lullaby and Jan sank into a bed of soft fern. There he fell asleep.

He was wakened by the caress of a soft hand upon his cheek.

"Come with me my son . . . for thou art my child now."

He gazed with wonder at the beautiful woman who had spoken. She took him by the hand and led him to the water's edge, but he tried to pull away as he realised where she was about to lead him.

Gathering him up into her arms, she walked out into the dark water.

"Have no fear, for thou art safe with me," she murmured.

The waters closed above their heads, the evening stars vanished and all was darkness.

His eyes opened to the shimmering reflections of a myriad rainbow crystals. A dazzling faerie kingdom lay beneath the lake. The lights that had lured him through the woods were carried by a moving host of faerie folk and it was their Queen who held him close. She laid him on a bed of silk and fed him upon new bread with honey, and creamy milk taken fresh from the cow.

"Thou shalt be mine," she said, holding him close, "if only for a little while, for thou art as like to my lost son as his reflection in a pool. Until the moon shall shine in full and darken once again, thou art my babe returned!"

So for a full month, while his true folk searched until all hope faded, Jan lived like a prince. On the day that the villagers dragged the dark lake, he played in the crystal halls below it with toys of gold.

When the moon was in her darkest quarter, a woodsman came upon the body of a child by the pool. He gently lifted the still figure, but then the boy stirred in his arms and cried to find himself in the cold darkness, away from the love and the light of the Faerie Queen.

In the following days he told as best he could, of the delights he had found beneath the lake, and in the following years would often return and sit at the pool side, listening for the enchanted music.

In time he grew and wed and moved far from the lake and the wood and thought no more of the beautiful Faerie Queen who had mothered him for a month.

But she watched over him every day of his life.

elisabeth foster

Faeries are of an ancient race,
their bloodline running thin.

The successful rearing of their own young through to healthy adulthood has long proved difficult, and the practice of utilising mortal foster mothers, whether willingly or by deception, has long been established.

The Faerie Nurseling

(Tom's Tale)

Tamsin Trevorrow worked from dawn 'til dusk to keep her cottage neat. The copper shone, the range was blacked, gingham curtains lifted in the fresh air that blew in from the west. Her chicks were plump, her cow was sleek and her man, Jack, never had a hole to his stocking.

Tamsin had all and every day to spare for housekeeping, for wed nearly seven years, she still had no child.

One fine spring morn as she hung her sheets out on the hedge to dry, she spied a stranger toiling up the hill. She didn't see whether he came from Zennor or St Ives. She ran inside and put the kettle on the fire to brew a dish of tea, then called the stranger in. He sat and drank and looked around, and while he admired the tabbiness of the cat and the pinkness of the geranium, she was noting the richness of his cloth and the fine lace kerchief in his hand.

"Tamsin Trevorrow," he said, at length, "I need a nursemaid for my child."

"But I am wed," said she, "I have a man and home to care for here."

"Tamsin Trevorrow, you have misunderstood me. I shall be gone away for several years, and I have been advised to leave my son with some good wife who may give him food and love and bring him forth to know what is right and what is wrong in this wicked world."

"Who gave you my name?" asked Tamsin, "Who sent you here to me?"

"Someone who knows you very well," the stranger replied with a broad smile, "someone who knows of your wifely ways and love of little ones. The wisest woman for many a mile has sent me to seek you out ... Mary Trelawney!"

Tamsin smiled in return. "The wisest woman in the world is indeed Mary Trelawney. She's my mother!"

"My folk often go to her for her good advice and clear counsel. So will you do me this service, Tamsin Trevorrow? I should pay you well."

With a flick of his kerchief the table was rolling with bright golden coins.

So a bargain was struck, and off went Tamsin with the stranger down the lane.

"I'm afraid you must be blindfolded for this part of the journey," and the stranger bound his kerchief about Tamsin's eyes. He guided her on gently, and she guessed that they had taken the turn onto the Zennor road. But soon they turned and climbed, and turned again and climbed again until she was bewildered. Then she heard a door creak open and they travelled somewhere dark, dank and cold beneath the ground.

At last they stopped and the blindfold was removed.

"Now you may look. But stop with me a while and eat, for I have tasted your hospitality, now you shall taste of mine."

Tamsin looked, her eyes and mouth wide open. She stood within a panelled hall before a great table set with silver. From one end to the other it was laden with roast meats, pies and pastries, soups and syllabubs, trifles and tarts. Decanters of fine wine and cut glass gleamed in the candlelight. Such a feast as she had ever seen, yet there were only places laid for two.

As they ate she slipped a few slices of meat into one pocket and a couple of the sweet tarts into

Elisabeth Foster

another for Jack's supper, for she was nothing if not thrifty.

"I'll fetch my son," her host declared after they had finished all that they could eat between them. He was not long gone, and returned bringing a tiny child wrapped in a cloth of fine white wool. The baby looked up at her with slanting blue eyes from beneath a fringe of golden curls and smiled. Tamsin took him in her arms and loved him from the start.

The stranger smiled.

"He will be yours until such time as I return, but these things you must remember. The child shall be washed but once a day, and only with the water which you shall find daily renewed in his room. Try not to touch the water, wear leather gloves and dry each splash away. Abide by this and you will always prosper."

So agreeing, Tamsin and the child were guided home.

Jack Trevorrow was a gentle man, and readily accepted their new charge.

Months passed, and the chid whom they called Tom grew well and happy. Tamsin washed him in the special water that was magically renewed each morning, careful not to wet her hands. Money for Tom's keep appeared magically on the mantle, and as the child grew, new clothes would be placed for him on his bed. Tamsin admired the fine stitching and the soft fabric, and marvelled at their perfect fit. At first she would take the outgrown clothes down to the market, (for she was nothing if not thrifty), riding proudly with little Tom on the fat pony that Tom's father's money had bought them. But word came back that the little garments had ruined at the first wash, with stitches as weak as cobwebs and weave as flimsy as gossamer. She sold no more, but left all the others to fade in a wooden chest.

Tom grew apace and learned to walk and run and play. He never seemed to be dirty at the end of a long day's tumbling in the yard. He was washed in the morning, his fair skin glowing almost gold, and was still as shining when the sun set.

Tamsin would watch him through the window as she set about her chores. He never seemed lonely as he leapt and climbed and chased around, chattering in his clear voice as if to a host of invisible companions.

The years passed and brought a brother and a sister for young Tom. He loved the babies, but even when they grew old enough to play with, he still seemed to prefer his own company, running and playing alone in the far fields. When little Will and baby Jenny tried to follow him, Tom would climb high into the trees, or disappear for hours on the hillside.

As the children grew older, so did Tamsin, and all the gold coins in the world could not stop the grey from growing at her temples, nor keep the lines from neck and brow. All the years of cleaning and caring for her family had roughened her once smooth skin.

One hot afternoon when Will and Jenny were with their father in the hayfield, Tamsin stood in Tom's room, gazing through his ever open window down into the yard. Tom sat talking to himself on the wall. Tamsin turned away, and sighed at her drab reflection in the tiny mirror on the wall. Her hands strayed to the white ewer on the table beside her, and cupping her palms, she scooped some of the precious water and splashed it on her face.

Wrinkles and lines faded like crumpled linen smoothed beneath a hot iron, her skin glowed like a young maid's at her first kiss, but her eyes stung badly where the water had splashed in.

She turned to the window, snatching at the curtain to wipe her eyes, then stopped and stared in amazement.

She could see Tom, still talking away, but now she could see Tom's companions. The little people sat along the wall and danced near the well, they climbed over the cow-house and rode the chickens across the yard. She gasped aloud as a little fellow

Elisabeth Foster

in green pulled the cat's whiskers whilst another stole its milk.

"Well, Tamsin Trevorrow, and what do you see?" said a voice behind her.

She turned to find the stranger from so many years before.

"I see that you have returned!" said she.

"If you can see me, then you can see what should be hidden!"

There was anger in his voice, and his face was grim.

"Do not be harsh, my husband." A gentle woman's voice came from the window, and there on the sill sat the most beautiful creature that Tamsin had ever seen. Perched happily on the narrow ledge beside her sat Tom.

"She has been a good mother to our child for these ten years. None of our own rearing has lived so long."

Then she spoke directly to Tamsin.

"It is time for the Prince to return to his Kingdom. We leave you with our thanks, and the blessings of our people."

Then she reached out and touched Tamsin's face with a slender finger.

"I'm afraid the lines will return in time, my dear, but only slowly."

Tamsin blinked as the gentle touch reached her eyes, the stinging was gone, but she could no longer see the Faerie King and Queen . . . or their child, her Tom.

At her feet lay the King's kerchief, and a final gift of gold. She put the money in her pocket and the kerchief in the wooden chest on top of the tiny clothes.

In time the cobweb stitches and the gossamer weave crumbled to dust.

Faerie-folk are essentially fair-minded and kind-hearted. If services are rendered, then payment is proffered, though usually in secret.

They do not welcome mortals learning of their good deeds, and sometimes such discoveries may cause any favours to abruptly cease.

Animals have no fear of the Little People, accepting them readily as part of the Natural World.

Faeries of the Field

(The Widow's Tale)

Luzelia Bowden had a fine cow. She didn't have much else, for the field and the cottage were tied to the Pascoe's Farm, and her husband was getting too sick for regular work. But Rosy, the vinny-cow gave rich milk twice daily which could be skimmed for the yellow butter and the scalded cream.

Every morning she would walk slowly down to market, and every noon she would walk slowly back again with a couple of pilchards or a rabbit for a pie.

Farmer Pascoe drove up the lane behind her one wet afternoon, forcing her against the soaking hedge. For a minute Luzelia thought that he might offer her a ride as his cart stopped beside her.

"Luzelia Bowden, you got a good cow there."

"Yes," she said, the rain dripping from her hair.

"I'll buy her from you. Give you a fair price."

"No, thank you, Mr. Pascoe," said Luzelia, "my cow's not for sale." And she walked on in the rain.

Soon John Bowden was too sick to work at all, then too sick to leave alone. Luzelia churned the butter and scalded the cream, but it was Tamsin Trevorrow's girl Jenny who took it to market.

On the night that Luzelia became Widow Bowden, Joe Pascoe came to her door.

"I'm sorry your man's gone, Luzelia, but I've a farm to work and the fields to plough. I'm going to need this cottage and the field beside it for the new man."

Luzelia wept anew.

A crafty look came into Pascoe's eyes. "I'll tell 'ee what, m'dear. I'm not a hard man. You shall stay on in the cottage, and the new man can board at the farm. I'll have to have the field cropping, so you let me have that milk-cow of yours in return. A better bargain you'll never find."

Luzelia could do nothing. She kept her home, but she lost her cow, and the best means to make a living.

It was a hard struggle, but she survived. She dug up the yard to plant potatoes and carrots, and travelled round about asking for people's washing and mending to do for the charge of a few pence.

One day when she was returning home with a full basket of mending to do from one of the big houses, she found a tiny shirt with a torn sleeve lying on the doorstep. Thinking it a child's, dropped from one of her bundles, she gathered it up and mended it with all the rest. Then noting that it was also badly stained, she laundered the tiny thing and left it overnight on the sill to dry.

In the morning it was gone, but there on the sill sat a good pound of yellow butter and a covered dish of cream, as good as ever came from Rosy.

The year turned on. Often Luzelia washed and mended some tiny garment, leaving it out on the sill to dry, and in the morning, butter, cream, or good fresh milk would be left in its place.

One afternoon in late summer, as she sat sunning herself with a dish of tea and a fresh bake of splits with jam and cream, old Dame Pascoe arrived at the door. Joe Pascoe's mother was a scold and a busybody. Some said she'd made Joe the man he was with her sharp tongue and penny-pinching ways.

Luzelia invited her in, offering tea and the splits fresh from the oven. The old woman accepted, checking the china for cracks and the bread for its texture. Then she spooned the cream and poured the milk and scraped the butter.

"Where do you come by such cream, milk and butter? she wanted to know, "we have none so fine.

Elisabeth Foster

That cow you gave my fool of a son for a lifetime's rent gives nothing at milking time, though her bag looks full."

"I get it where I can find it," said Luzelia, "and as for the cow, perhaps she misses the good grass from the field out there."

She looked out of the window to where Rosy's old pasture had been dug over and planted with turnips.

The old woman followed her gaze.

"They'll be a goodly crop of turmots there," she said, "and don't you go helping yourself. That's not your field no longer, and this shouldn't still be your cottage by rights . . . that cow's no good, and she'll be away to the market for meat next week!"

Luzelia looked upset at this, but the old woman pressed on.

"Perhaps that's where your cream and butter come from, Widow Bowden, could be that you creeps up the hill of an evening with your bucket and helps yourself to what is mine!"

"All that saves you from being thrown headlong through that window," said Luzelia, "is that you are the oldest, as well as the sourest body that I know. Get out of my house!"

Mrs Pascoe left, grumbling all the way to the gate.

"I'll have you sent packing to the poorhouse!" she threatened, "I'll have it put about town and village that you're both thief and liar . . . I'll tell all my friends to tell their friends . . . "

"You have no friends!" shouted Luzelia, "Nor never had!" and shut the window.

That night she retired late to her bed, all mending finished, all laundry dried on the hedge. She had just blown out the candle when there was a great knocking at the door. Fearing some intruder, or perhaps another visit from Dame Pascoe or her son, she fetched the brass knobbed poker and shouted through the window to know who was there.

"Let me in, Mrs Bowden, let me in! I must see you, let me in!"

There stood young Annie, Joe Pascoe's daughter left motherless from birth and used like a skivvy by the old woman. Annie was in a rare state, half laughing and half crying, her bare feet grass stained and her hair wild as a bird's nest.

"Come in and sit down, child, you're fair mazed. Tell me what's to do."

Soon Annie was curled up in the big old chair, wrapped in a shawl with a hot drink to hold. Annie took a good sip and started her tale.

"Well, father's gone up the hill a while since and never come down again, though we've searched high and low. Gramma's on and on about milk being taken from the cow, and set me to sitting out in the field all night without even a lantern to see who comes to take it . . . "

"And did anyone come?"

"Only Will Trevorrow," said Annie, blushing prettily, "and that to keep me company. He didn't think it fitty for a maid to wait all alone, by herself in a dark field 'til sun-up".

"Did you see anyone else?" said Luzelia.

"Yes," said Annie, "I'll tell you. Will was there before the sun went down, and he picked me some lovely posy from the hedge, and he found me a four-leaf grass for good fortune, see . . ." She drew from her pocket a crumpled nosegay of wildflowers and a flattened four-leaved clover.

"That's what did it! Will told me we would see all the hidden things if we held it in our hands between us . . . and we did! There stood your Rosy, standing happy in the long grass, then we see a troupe of the Little People, coming from all around with clover flowers in their hands. There was a boy there, a bit bigger than the rest, with a pail of shining gold. Will was most taken with the boy, swearing him to be the image of the brother he lost as a lad. He was in a fair sweat about that and would have run off home, but I held onto him."

Luzelia's cat leapt up onto Annie's lap, making her jump.

"Go on," said Luzelia, "what happened next?"

"The boy milked the cow. You should have seen the streams of good milk that went into that golden bucket, and I could never get the old girl to let down a drop! Then the Little Folk dipped their flowers into the bucket, brought them out and sucked them dry, then dipped and sucked again and again. By this time the sun was setting, and the boy turned to us, his face all gold in the last of the light.

"Will," he said, "tell mother that her boy Tom has not forgotten her."

At this, Will shouted and dropped the clover and we saw no more?"

Luzelia took the kettle from the hob and brewed more tea whilst Annie looked sleepily into the fire.

"Where have you been since, my girl? The sun set hours gone."

"Will saw me back home, and then I had to wake Gramma and tell her all that I'd seen, except that I didn't talk of Will's being there with me!"

"And what did Dame Pascoe have to say?"

"She cried and she cursed, and she named you a witch woman. She declared that you've set the Little People against her and had them steal away her son. She says that you've overlooked both cow and crop and that nothing will ever go right with her again. She turned her shift to keep the Little Folk away from her . . . but best of all, she declares that she won't come out of her room 'til father be found."

But Farmer Pascoe was never found, and the old Dame stayed in her room. Annie ran the farm as best she could, but returned the field and Rosy the cow to the Widow Bowden.

The Little People no longer came to milk the cow now that Luzelia had her home again, but still on occasions the tiny torn garments were left on her step, and she would mend and wash them. Her payment came now in the form of hedgerow fruit or posies of wild-flowers, for Rosy gave her all the milk and cream and butter she could ever need, and more than enough besides to take down to the market.

Faeries have a love of justice and a hatred of human greed, although their own faults appear to be pardonable.

Although their world remains mostly invisible to human eyes, certain tested charms and spells will prove potent in enabling ordinary folk to observe them. However, any that do so with grasping or evil intent should beware, as faeries can sense such desire and their reaction may be swift and unpleasant.

The Faerie Hill
(The Miser's Tale)

Joe Pascoe was as turned and twisted inside as the wind-bent trees that sprouted from the hedges of his fields. As a child he shared with no-one; such treats and sweetmeats that came his way were to be savoured in secret, alone in his room.

The only joy of his life had also been a private mystery; he'd returned from a trip to an up-country town with a frail and pretty wife. For a brief year the world saw another Joe. This man had a proud smile, time to stop for a drink and a chat. He was even known to buy a round. He whistled around the farm, and spent a season with the choir. Then his wife died in childbirth, leaving him a lusty daughter with good lungs and a great appetite. His mother grudgingly helped him rear the child, but all his love had blown out like a candle at his wife's death, and he hated the world once more.

If someone had anything that Joe Pascoe wanted, he'd move Heaven and Earth to get it, and when he'd got it he'd gloat for weeks on end until he set his heart on another field, or a neighbour's cart, or even a plough that seemed to furrow straighter than his own. Not that Joe couldn't have bought new what he needed, for he spent little enough of what he hoarded. His delight was in acquiring those things that others valued, preferably at the least possible cost.

One August night Joe Pascoe stood in one of his fields looking down on his farm. It was a fine, clear night with a sickle moon, and from where Joe stood all that he could see belonged to him. Then he turned his back on what was his own, and looked up at the hill.

He hated the hill. No-one seemed to know who owned it, no-one grazed it. Some said it was haunted and others said it had always been the home of the Fair Folk and was thus held sacred. It was now the only thing that Joe Pascoe could see from his window that he did not own. It rose against the sky and defied him daily.

Now he'd found out what he must do, and if the Fair Folk dwelt there in truth, he would seek them out and strike a bargain with them for their home.

The night had come, there was little light, but Joe could manage without. He'd walked this path so many times that the grass was flattened. Nearly to the top went Joe, to where a great boulder lay, half hidden in the bracken, carelessly tossed there by the giants of a bygone age. Beside the boulder was a dip in the earth where the sun never reached and the star-moss grew. There he listened for the pounding and the piping to begin, deep within the ground. Then nine times against the sun, Joe walked round the hill-top. He paused for a moment, then scrambled up to the top of the great stone and waited in the dark.

A strip of light appeared in the ground below him, and the hillside opened. Crowds of little people poured forth from the hollow hill and set about preparing a great feast. Tables were set up, and plate was set out of silver and of gold. Jewelled lamps were placed in the bracken and on the stones, until the hillside glimmered like a great glittering jewel.

After the tiny people came the ugly and deformed from their holes and passageways beneath the earth; the knockers from the mines; the bucca-bos from their sea-caves; the spriggans from their standing stones. Then the sprites and piskies from the fields and farms came bounding up through the bracken and heather. More slowly and more silently

Elisabeth Foster

appeared the dwellers of the rocks and trees, still water and river spirits and the child spirits that played forever. Finally came the Fair Folk themselves, tall and graceful, winged women and stern men, proud, beautiful and sometime cruel.

All took their places for the feast while Joe Pascoe looked down upon them.

The King stood and raised high his golden goblet.

"Are we all met?" he cried, in a mighty voice.

"Our number is not yet quite complete, my Lord!" The voice came from beside Joe's head, and a slender woman in grey and silver rose from the very rock on which he lay. "There is one here who has no seat at our table. I'll bring him to you."

She clasped him with a grip of granite and brought him struggling before the King.

"Come, join us at our Feasting," welcomed the King, though his eyes were hard and cold. "We have long felt your hunger in the air around us. Come! Bring forth the baked and the sweet that our honoured guest may dine!"

Joe shook his head. He knew enough of Faerie-lore to refuse any refreshment, lest he be enchanted and enslaved for all time.

The King shrugged. "So be it. But having decided to come amongst us this night, you will stay and share our revels!"

At a signal from their King, a thousand laughing sprites or more dashed forward and bound Joe from head to foot with webs of silk which held him fast upon the ground.

All through the long night he stayed bound, watching the feasting, the carefree singing and wild dancing on the hillside. A constant stream of Little People came to him with drink and food, at first offering it with smiles and winning gesture, but on his refusal they would push the food against his mouth or throw the drink in his face with spite and gleeful malice.

He fought to keep his lips closed against the pulling of little fingers, clenching his teeth against the intruding claws.

In the dark hour before dawn he found his torment over. The lights dimmed, the music faded into silence and he found himself alone beneath the sky. He was still trussed and tied by the fine strands, his mouth dry and parched and his jaw ached from being clenched shut for so long.

He closed his tired eyes, and seemed to see his dead wife. In her hand she held a ripe peach, the flesh new bitten, the juice trickling between her fingers.

Kneeling beside him she held the fruit gently to his mouth. He bit into it, and the moist flesh disolved into a liquid sweetness that drenched his mouth and throat.

There was a peal of laughter and a flood of light, he opened his eyes wide in horror to see the woman who had taken him from the rock kneeling at his side. On the glowing hillside stood the Faerie Host, clapping, cheering, laughing, jeering . . .

The King stepped forward.

"We have long felt your greed and your desire, it radiates from you like a furnace throwing heat. You want our hill, our home, our last haven in this land. You thought perhaps to bargain with us, to buy something that cannot be had for gold. But now you have eaten of our enchanted fruit you have joined the ranks of the Immortal. I welcome you to our realm, and I can appease your hunger for our hill. Thus I give it to you. Forever."

He signalled once more to his subjects.

Joe Pascoe felt the tug of every strand that held him fast. The pulling was unbearable. He felt that he was upon a giant's rack as the shimmering web pulled him away into the darkness. He was being stretched uphill and down, around the hill and over its summit. From above, the rocks and trees moved to bury him, from below the hands and fingers from within dragged him down. He heard and saw no more.

Quietly, as the sun rose, the Fair Folk journeyed home, and within the very centre of the hill, slowly beat Joe Pascoe's heart of stone.

The most ancient of the faerie lines inhabit the very trees, plants and stones of the earth.

They form the essential spirit of the natural substance, and in the past have often been worshipped as such.

They may wander freely, but become desperate if taken by accident or design from their natural home.

The Faerie of the Wood
(Will's Tale)

Will's dreams had troubled him ever since he had repaired the boat. From the time he'd cut and shaped the wood for the new bowsprit, his sleeping hours had been plagued. He saw visions of a woman who stood before him, her green gown moulded to her slim figure, eyes wide, hands raised, she implored him, she beseeched him . . . but her voice was ever silenced by the rising of the wind.

His time ashore was over; the nets were mended, the new bowsprit was in place and the boat ready to sail. Will kissed his sweetheart, farewell and went aboard with the rest of the crew.

They sailed out of the harbour before a westerly breeze and fished well beyond the reef. The weather was fine, the sea calm and the shoals just where they expected to find them. They returned their catch to the shore, then the skipper took them straight out again. Once more their luck held, and as Will hauled on the bulging nets, he dreamed of telling Annie about the catch, and planning the fine wedding they could have with the money he'd made.

Then their luck changed. The wind veered and brought a great storm boiling out of the north-west. Day was turned to night by the dark clouds racing over the sky and great seas rose with white caps that flew before them in the wind.

Will was sent forward as look-out, to the bow, clinging to the bowsprit as the waves curled and broke above him. As his hands gripped the newly varnished wood he saw through the crashing waters that he was not alone.

Perched out on the thin spar was the woman from his dreams, her gown torn and ragged in the storm winds, her dark hair streaming about her shoulders.

The skipper was trying to hold their course for the harbour, but the savage winds drove their boat towards the reef and the sea tossed it upon the rocks like a discarded toy. With a grinding of shattering timbers, the boat and crew were lost; all but Will who clung in desperation to the new bowsprit he had fashioned only days before. Drifting in and out of consciousness, dazed with shock and numb from cold, he was tossed and battered by the waves, the rocks, and the wreckage.

"Swim!", came a voice in his ear, "Kick out for your life, and I can guide us to the shore."

Crouched above him, balancing on the slippery wood, was the woman in green.

Will kicked out, feebly at first, then with determination. They bobbed with the broken wood and tangled ropes of the wreck, driven forward by the surging waves as the storm lessened and the night fell.

Will had never been so tired, his strength was gone and he was sick with swallowed water.

"Don't stop, you fool, we're nearly there!"

A sharp slap across his cheek and the hissing voice in his ear brought him fully awake once more. He could see the woman, in spite of the night's darkness, for her skin shone with a green glow and her eyes were shining points of emerald fire.

"Listen!" she cried.

He could hear the sound as the great waves broke upon the shore. He gave just a few more kicks, then a vast wall of water rose from beneath him and carried him far up upon the beach.

He lay for a while and caught his breath, then looked about him for the woman, but she was not there. His search took him to the water's edge, where the tumbling surf tossed the bowsprit to his

Elisabeth Foster

feet. Remembering the hours of work that he had put into its shaping, he hauled it from the water with the last of his strength and staggered with it beyond the high water mark. There he fell into the wet sand and wept, mourning his comrades who had perished and the woman who had driven him to save himself from the sea.

She came to him in his dreams as he lay, smiling, arms outstretched. She kissed him, and he held her in his arms, and they lay together on the sand.

When he awoke, the sun was high and he lay in a familiar cove, and he was clutching the bowsprit in a close embrace.

A farmer with a cart helped Will back to his home, the bowsprit riding with him. He felt now that he knew its secret, and the next day he had it taken back to the woods from whence it came. He propped it near the tree-stump that still stood with the sawdust round it, and there he waited for the night.

As the moon rose, she came walking through the trees.

"You caught me sleeping within the very wood when first you cut this tree. Trapped there I could not escape and was shaped beneath your hands with the biting edge of tools and the stench of oil and varnish. How I hated you! I came to you nightly, and implored you to set me free. But finally it was your strength that brought me to the shore. Now that you have brought me home I can hate you no more, for I might have ridden the seas forever, or else sunk and rotted with the ship. For my glad homecoming I thank you."

Will tried to apologise and thank her all in the same breath, but she laughed at his stuttering speech and silenced him with a kiss.

Taking him by the hand she led him amongst the trees until they came to a toppled oak.

"Now, take your wood only from such trees as have fallen in the storms, for no spirits dwell within them. Then shall you build a fine boat and harvest the sea."

She kissed him again and held him to her.

"But now, my Will, I shall tell you this . . . I have made you mine. Forsake me for any other and I swear by every tree that grows in this land, I shall come to you nightly and ride your dreams forever!"

Will gave his Annie not a second thought as he took the hand of the woman all in green, and they walked together into the darkness of the wood.

Faeries

do not welcome trespassers into their special places. They often work hard to protect what is their own, and like many rare species they may face extinction as unknowing humans reach at last into all the remote and forgotten corners of the land.

The Faerie Garden
(The Tale of Jan and his Jenny)

Winter had lain across the country like an iron hand, with hard ground and whitened stalks and brown stems rotting. The change of season brought only the harsh winds from the sea, bending the gnarled trees further, sending the salt spray across the stony fields.

Jan went about his work with a heavy heart. From field to field his small crop was dying in the thin soil. Down in the harbour the boats would not dare venture out, no catches were landed and the price of corn was high.

At home his Jenny sat in her seat by the meagre fire, her cheeks pale and her fingers thin as they pulled her wrap closer around. The short days and the long nights passed, and still the winds blew. The cottage seemed to shake with every wave that curled and crashed on the cliffs below.

Jenny's mind seemed to wander, happier in the times when she and Jan had walked the cliffs in summers past.

"Jan, Jan, pick me some flowers! The cliffs are all pink with them growing in the little gardens . . . Jan, pick me some sea pink for my hair."

"There are no flowers yet, my love. In a month or so I'll walk the lanes and find you cowslip and heartsease, and the bluebells to match your eyes."

"I want to see the sea pinks growing," whispered Jenny, "in the gardens on the cliffs once more."

Jan leaned his great fork against the rough stone wall and looked out over the sea. The wind had blown a hole in the sky, and through the cloud a pool of sunlight lay across the water and over the cliff tops to his feet. A flash of colour caught his eye, and stepping carefully he went to the edge of the rocks and looked over. There, in the sheltered places between the cairns, there were patches of new and brilliant green, and in one of them the budded tufts of sea-pink nodded their bright heads.

Over the edge went Jan, swinging down from handhold to foothold, until one rock, weakened by the winter frosts, crumbled free beneath his fingers. He fell, and caught, and fell again, then grasped once more, holding and hanging above the pounding sea. The little flowers nodded, inches from his face.

Then tiny people moved out from behind the stones, behind the green tufts, from within the cracks of the cliff itself. They lined up on the rocks, regarding him with solemn faces. Each one held a small weapon; club, spear or sword, poised above Jan's clutching fingers.

"Why do you come to our private gardens, clumsy mortal?" enquired an ancient greybeard in squeaky tones. "No-one of your kind shall trespass unscathed in our domain. Before we send you tumbling to the water, tell us what you seek here at the Land's End."

"Flowers!" gasped Jan, "I only wanted flowers."

The needle points of sword and spear pricked the skin of his fingers, the little clubs were raised, and the old one spoke again.

"Why should you want to plunder our first harvest of the year? Why should you take from us the first, sweet nectar that we have nurtured through winter's long, dark days?"

Jan knew fear, but he also then knew anger. Would these tiny beings cut at his fingers until he fell to the waves below? Would his Jenny be left to sorrow and sicken in their cottage alone, and perhaps lose the child that they awaited?

"I wanted them for Jenny!" he cried, "For Jenny

Elisabeth Foster

who puts the first cream of the milking out on the sill for you each morn. For Jenny who cuts the first slice of the new batch for you on baking day and leaves it on the stile. For Jenny, who does not let you hunger, even in a winter such as this. So cut away my fingers, see me fall, and let Jenny's heart be broken . . . for she is already sick and like to die."

Then the little folk moved foward, from beside, above, below. Jan was seized and born back to the cliff top, to the very wall of his own field.

As he lay trying to catch his breath, a bunch of sea-pink was placed in his hand, and a woman's voice whispered gently in his ear.

"Thrift stands for sympathy. We hope that we have not used you ill. Take the flowers for your Jenny."

Jan forgot his fork and stumbled home across the fields. Smoke from his cottage chimney billowed across the grey land and the sky was dark once more. But inside his home all was warmth and light. His Jenny came laughing to greet him, catching him at the door with a kiss. Pulling him inside she skipped around the room, and everywhere, glowing in the warm firelight were the flowers. In every cloam pot, in every cooking pan, in every cup, bucket and tankard were bluebells, hyacinths, daffodils, narcissus, wild anemone and primrose, honeysuckle and white-briar. Every scent hung in the air like summer, and all colour was there, save one. The only pink blooms were clutched tight in Jan's hand.

Jan held Jenny close and handed her the thrift that had near cost him so dear.

"And these, my love, are for your hair."

In the long summer evenings that came at last, they sat and nursed the new baby, high on the cliff tops amid the samphire and wild thyme. Above the rumbling of the steady waves, they fancied they could hear the singing of the little folk as they tended their gardens far below.

And the Faerie Queen watched over them, then as always.

The fair folk are a people of tradition and ceremony, slow to accept any change.

They can be proud and willful, unable to adapt and utilise new ideas.

This stubborn approach has led to the dwindling of their numbers and even to their total disappearance in some places.

Faerie Fortune
(The Wise Woman of Wendron)

It was after the Lammastide Festival, when the Fair Folk had danced night into day and back again. The usual few mortals had crept around on the hillside trying to have a geek, and there had been quite a lot of competition among the younger, more mischievous sprites, spriggans and piskies as to who could cast the most amusing spell to ensnare them.

An elderly lady with eyes only for the gold plate set at the tables had been turned into an earthenware jug, and a young drunkard (obviously there for a bet with his friends), had been set to dancing all night with a scarecrow which he believed to be a winsome maid.

Two lovers on the far side of the hill were rescued by the faeries from any such merry jests, as it was obvious from the start that their appearance in the festivities was accidental. Sending the pranksters packing, the Faerie Queen herself turned the entwined couple into a pair of decently feathered doves encased in a firmly built bower which kept them safely out of the way for the duration.

Now the wild dancing and the full feasting was done. The earthenware jug had gone back to her home, much chastened, the drunkard lay in some far field, snoring happily in the arms of his beloved scarecrow and the love birds had flown.

The Queen of Faerie sat on a tussock and spoke with the High King of All Spriggans.

"It's not working," quoth the High King (he often quothed).

"I'm afraid you're right," agreed the Queen. "I think the time has come to approach the Wise Woman."

It had seemed like a good idea at the time. Given the fact that their numbers were dwindling, and too few little ones were born to any of the Fair folk, the King of All Spriggans and the Queen of Faerie decided that two of their kind should wed. It was hoped that this unlikely union would strengthen their stock and bring forth a new race of sturdy but beautiful beings endowed with all the best in both races. Unfortunately the happy couple selected for this experiment loathed each other.

The wedding had taken place twelve months before, with the greatest feasting and frolicking seen in many a long age, but now, one year later, Clawfingers had sat with a group of young Spriggans drinking himself insensible, whilst the beautiful Saxifrage had stayed with a group of her friends, swapping make-up tips and discussing the horrors of her married life. They had left the gathering separately.

The next day the Queen dragged them both off to consult the Wise Woman of Wendron. As they approached her cottage they could hear clearly her dispensing her good advice to someone through the opened windows.

"You be sick as a gurnet, my bird, and deef as a haddick, and you don't need that no more than a toad needs side-pockets. You're lookin' like a stewed owl. Now then, take a spoonful of earth from the grave of a newly burrid virgin, dissolve it in water and drink it fasting to cure the decline. Next!!!"

They went in, and there, seated around the stained, bare table, they discussed their problem.

"I hate him!" cried Saxi, "He is brutish and ugly. He cares nothing for the beauty of light on the sea, or the tonal qualities of a good rainbow. He doesn't appreciate the work I do amongst the flowers, he

Elisabeth Foster

won't eat the nectar I bring in for him. He can't fly, and he works nights!"

"Well at least I work!" hissed the Spriggan. "I should have married a lass who had the strength to shift stones and the patience to guard treasure. Someone who might have cleaned the place up once in a while and bake toad the way I like it." He glared at her, ". . . and she has these headaches!"

The Wise Woman nodded thoughtfully, "Scritchin' at each other like a pair of whitnicks," she said, scratching the hairs on her chin, "they that can't schemey must louster."

"I beg your pardon?" murmured the Queen.

"As I see it, a change of work is as good as a tich-pipe, and this'll fit like a stocking on a man's nose."

She sent Clawfingers and Saxifrage outside and had a word in private with the Queen.

"I got the wisdom, but you got the magic, sure as red-haired people can never make good butter. Let's switch 'em around, let 'un learn what it is to appreciate one's strength and t'other's beauty."

The Queen led her sulking subjects to a clearing amongst the gnarled and moss-barked trees.

"You shall dwell within this sylvan glade for one week," pronounced the Queen.

"Doesn't look much like a sylvan glade to me . . ." muttered Saxi.

"Shut up and listen to the Queen when she's pronouncing!" growled Clawfingers.

The Queen glared at both of them.

"Here shall you undergo a testing of your spirits, and learn an understanding of each other. Now you, Yellow Bog Saxifrage . . . " (this was her full name and she hated it) ". . . can you weave?"

"Yes, your Majesty," said Saxi, somewhat surprised.

"Then in the next seven days you shall weave a mantle of such unsurpassed loveliness for your husband that he will treasure it forever."

"Er, what out of?" said Saxi, looking round hopefully for a loom and a few good skeins of silk.

"From a basic diet of flies, creepy crawlies and other such dainties!" With that, the Queen turned her into a large hairy spider.

"In this form you shall learn the value of strength and hard work, and that being beautiful isn't everything."

Then she turned to Clawfingers, who stood with his mouth open, displaying a fine set of fangs.

"You, Dread Clawfingers of the Night, shall learn to live on a diet of nectar, appreciate flowers and enjoy seven day's worth of flying. Perhaps you might learn of the qualities possessed by your wife that you are unable to understand."

With a twirl of her long fingers the Queen turned him into a gorgeous butterfly.

It was a strange week. Saxi climbed and scuttled and spun her first web, (which promptly broke the first time she sat on it.) It was hard work, catching dinner, parcelling it up tidily and hanging it in the larder. Although distasteful at first, she soon found a dark joy in subduing her prey and mastering even the hugest of bluebottles with her great hairy legs. The web had to be constantly repaired, the strands checked for the correct tension and firm anchorage.

And she had to weave the mantle. Because she built her webs low, fearing the heights without her familiar wings, she discovered the delights of the more earthy colours, browns, rusts, moss green and indigo shades. The silken cloth grew daily, glowing with the subtle, secret colours of the shaded grove. Although she did finish off the collar later in gold lamé with a magenta fleck.

Meanwhile she saw little of Clawfingers. He rose each day with the sun, spreading his glowing wings in the warmth, soaring above the trees and away to the meadow. He quickly learned which flowers held the sweetest nectar, following the bright guidelines which led to the delicious heart of each bloom. He practised the delicate manipulation of his long proboscis, and the infinite care needed to untangle

Elisabeth Foster

his legs in a high wind. But most of all, he learned to love his wings.

Velvet soft to fold at night, cool as satin in the sun, with glorious colour and precise pattern, they lifted him with thoughtless ease above the earth and into the summer sky. He preened them, and polished them, and removed any stray pollen grain with a dainty kick. But, apart from an unfocussed squint over his back, he could never, ever, see them.

On the seventh day he landed lightly beside his toiling wife. She was just finishing her task, tidying away the odd snippets of silk, and wondering whether the mantle would wash best at a low temperature with few suds . . .

They stood and stared at one another, and in the many mirrors of her many eyes, at last Clawfingers saw his wings.

"Beautiful," he breathed, "truly beautiful."

Saxi naturally thought he was looking at her mantle.

"Thank you," she said shyly.

The Faerie Queen arrived just in time to hear the exchange. She smiled upon them, turned them back into their rightful forms, and smiled as they fell into each other's arms.

It all seemed to have worked very well. Clawfingers was a bit too embarrassed to wear the mantle in public, saving it only for night time dances, but they decided that it made a very spectacular bed-cover.

When their first child arrived, they asked the Wise Woman to the Name-Feast. She brought them a house-leek to grow on the roof and ward off the lightning, and blessed the new baby, or Friggan as they called him. He had long strong fingers and tiny, soft crumpled wings.

Late into the night, Mary Trelawny, the Wise Woman of Wendron danced on and on with the Lord of all Spriggans.

"You be graffled up like an airish pig!" she whispered in his ear.

He blushed in the moonlight.

"I hope that I might be able to say the same of you, good lady," he softly replied, "will you be my wife?"

And so the stock of any race may be strengthened with true love and understanding.

Every dweller in the faerie Kingdom is a lover of music and an active participant in any dance. Their music may enchant and ensnare any mortal that may hear it, and those lucky enough to dance with the fair folk seldom remain unchanged.

Changed too are those mortals that fall in love with a faerie.

Faerie Lover
(The Dancing Stone)

Annie peeped from the small upstairs window, watching as one and all stepped out to the Feast. In bright dresses and shining shoes, ribbons and buckles and bows, Sunday best and summer clothes to dance by torchlight on the green.

"Annie!" came her Gramma's cry, "'tis time you fetched home the cow and got me my supper!"

So Annie fetched home the cow, and brought bread and fresh milk and cheese from the slab to her Gramma's room.

"May I go to the dancing?" pleaded Annie. "I've mother's dress to wear, my good shoes are polished, and all my work is done."

"What if I should cry out in the dark and no-one to hear me?" moaned the old woman. "I could die in the night, in the dark, all alone. You killed your poor mother coming into this world, and you'll not drive me out of it with your wicked ways. We're together, you and I, since your father's gone, and you'll not leave me alone . . . "

The salt tears ran down her wrinkled face and dribbled through the whiskers on her chin.

Later, much later, as the old woman's snoring grumbled through the walls, Annie crept to the chest in the hall where her mother's dress lay with rosemary and lavender lingering in its folds. But the chest was open and the dress gone. Annie searched upstairs and down, while the music from the green called her to the dance.

She quietly entered the old woman's room. In the fusty darkness the snores drowned the music, but by the light of her shielded candle, Annie found her dead mother's dress. Gramma slept with it in the bed, her head pillowed on flowers embroidered so long ago. Her knobbled fingers were locked tight around Annie's polished shoes.

In her cotton shift, with bare feet, Annie slipped through the dark fields and up onto the hill. She could hear the music and the laughing and see the figures far below. She danced in the grass with the memory of her lost love that never returned to her from the sea, turning and swaying, arms wide and hair flying.

In the darkness she felt a strong arm grip her waist, and a brown hand held hers. For a moment she thought it Will, but the voice was not his.

"Will thou dance with me, fair maid?" His voice was soft and low.

His fine blonde hair was banded with gold, his clothes of silk and velvet, his smile was as secret as the sickle moon and his eyes were the blue of midnight.

Now other dancers were appearing on the hill, and their own musicians moved amongst them, players with lute and pipe and fiddle. Ladies in satin and ivory lace, with gossamer wings whirled and spun with Lords near as finely garbed as Annie's partner.

The music grew shrill and faster. Now they danced in the air, above the crags and standing stones. On the earth beneath them the torches were put out and mortal folk went happily home to bed, but still Annie danced on, held in the arms and heart of her new love. Above the hill and beneath the stars they kissed, and all below was silence, save for the cries of Gramma as she called out in the dark.

As the night faded and light came gently to the sky, the dancers fell slowly to the ground. Like night mists that disappear into the day, they were swallowed into air and stone and earth.

Elisabeth foster

Annie stood alone with her Faerie Prince.

"Shall I dance with you again?" she asked, breathless and laughing.

"Only if you promise to await me here."

"I'll wait!" cried Annie, "I'll wait for you forever!"

"Then I shall seal that promise with a kiss."

As the first light of the sun rose above the hill he kissed her full on the lips, and there stood Annie, turned to stone.

But beside her stands another stone, and when the time is right and the music plays, Annie and Tomàs dance forever on the hill.

There is a belief that faeries
are the unclaimed souls of
children, full of fun and mischief,
earthbound for eternity.

Others believe them to be lost spirits
tied to the land by natural forces,
forever bonded to the places
that they have loved the best in life.

The Faerie Circle

(Dicky Danjy's Holt)

The old man picked his way carefully across the slippery rocks. He paused now and again to lift the fronds of seaweed away from the pools to look at the small crabs that scuttled across the pebbles and back into the shelter of the stones. Gulls screamed and wheeled above him, but he ignored them for at this end of his life he found it much easier to look down than up.

Long ago he'd skipped across these very rocks with ease, defying the waves that plunged about them, always the last of the children racing to the safety of the cliffs where they'd watched the tide flowing in. But now he was alone, and the tide was ebbing fast.

He started as the calling of the seabirds echoed the voices of his memory. It had sounded like his name, called out from beneath the cliff, but when he looked there was nothing but the dark rocks and the moving birds.

Unsteadily he made his way across the stones, stopping as once again a sweet high voice seemed to cry out his name. This time, peering with the misty vision of the old, he saw a movement against the darkness of the cliff. It looked like a child that stood there, calling and beckoning him onward.

Now he knew exactly where he was, and clear recollection, much better than his sight brought back a summer seventy years long gone.

"Doan 'ee go in Dicky Danjy's Holt. The fairies'll take ee!"

So the mothers of the village children warned them. The dark cave and the treacherous sea were not enough to keep the young from straying, so the women had warned of the Fairy Folk who gathered unwary children into the cave to play forever at the sea's edge.

Jacky and his friends cared little about the fairies, and didn't fear the sea. They were immortal, climbing, running, leaping, diving, swimming where they liked; always coming home safe to a meal and a warm bed.

Their wild ways were curbed for a month or more in the year that the storms took the boat belonging to Rob Polglase's father, and young Rob with it. Then after a while they'd talked of Rob no more, just as they no longer talked of Sam and Betty Pender who died of the lung fever two winters before, though their sad mother still waited at the school-house to see them come home.

The old man rested himself upon a flat rock, as the long forgotten names and faces flowed into his mind. Perhaps this had been the very rock he'd waited on before, on the clear September night when he'd first known fear. Not that the others had known about that, for he'd been alone then, as now.

His dare had been to wait at Dicky Danjy's. To climb inside the cave after the tide had turned, and see if the fairies would come and take him.

He could have read by the strong light of the moon as he'd waited, if he had been the kind to have carried a book. The light seemed doubled by the silver on the sea. The water washed back and away, and waiting in the cold and damp of the night, Jacky had wished more than once for the warmth of his bed. The moon slowly lowered and shone full in the cave, and there he saw them, of moonlight and sea spray, dancing from the shadows like graceful children with eyes of cold silver. And there in the dancing was Rob, who was lost with his father, and Samuel and Betty that lay in the churchyard.

Elisabeth Foster

They called to Jacky with hands out and empty eyes.

"Jackee, Jackeeee, come here and join us, and we'll play forever. There's a place waiting for you, inside Dicky Danjy's . . . "

Up the cliff like a goat had run Jacky Trevorrow. Through the brightness and darkness of moon-shadowed houses, up the pipe by the window and under the bedclothes, weeping to have looked upon those things that couldn't have been.

In the morning he'd told of nothing but the waiting and the cold, and perhaps an owl that had called, but nothing of those things which couldn't have been.

In time he believed his own story.

But now he sits on the rock and remembers, as the sun goes down, the full moon comes to the sky behind him, and his last tide turns.

No more can he run from the dancing shadows of silver that now come to claim him . . . he's the last of them all. Here's Tom Penhallow that went for a soldier, and John and Saul Hocking that farmed up to Madron and Patience Trevoase that wed Ben from Newlyn. Standing out in the front is his lost wife Tamsin, as young as the day they'd played in the meadow, and he'd brought a blush to her cheek with the first kiss of many.

Now they're all waiting, all calling for Jacky, the fearless, who'd run home weeping from Dicky Danjy's Holt.

"Jackeeee, Jackeeee . . . get up and join us. It's time for the playing, the dancing, the climbing. Jackeee, Jackeee, we've kept your place waiting these many long years. Now the time's come to join us . . . come to Dicky Danjy's."

Young Jacky rises from the rock, and runs to join them, leaping through the rising waves that topple the old man's body into the sea.

... and some just believe in fairies

Elisabeth Foster

BIBLIOGRAPHY

The Faerie Circle

Source Material

"Mythology of the British Isles"
Ashe, Geoffrey.
Methuen. 1990.

"Traditions and Hearthside Stories of West Cornwall"
Bottrell, W.
Llanerch Enterprises. 1989

"Cornish Sayings, Superstitions and Remedies"
Hawke, Kathleen.
Lodeneck Press. 1973.

"Cornish Folk-Lore"
Hunt, Robert.
Tormark Press. 1988.

"In Search of Lost Gods"
Whitlock, Ralph.
Phaidon Press. 1979.